AF421692

THE WAR OF BELIEF

A BRIEF CHURCH HISTORY

STEVEN CAPRIGLIONE

Steven Capriglione
sjcapriglione@gmail.com
stevencapriglione.wordpress.com

To Adrian. Thank you for the idea of the title and may the Lord use this little book to help you as you grow in the faith once delivered.

INTRODUCTION

Growing up, the idea of studying church history was usually frowned upon by those in the churches I attended. Much like modern history, it was disregarded as what has been said and done. "Look to the future!" But, also like modern history, when we do not learn from our past, we are often doomed to repeat the tragedies of the past. R. C. Sproul once said that if Christians would just read a book on the history of the church we could avoid many of the problems that plague the church today.

And it is with this in mind that I wanted to write this book. It is no hyperbole that there is an ongoing war against Christianity. Sometimes this war rages within the visible church—consider the ongoing trouble between Protestants and Catholics or Reformed ideologies and those represented by the Charismatic Movement. Sometimes, these wars are waged with those outside the visible church, namely from the atheistic or postmodernistic person. They attempt to attack the credibility Scripture, repudiate our stances on moral issues, and work to get us to bend to their ungodly will.

This book covers both aspects. Here, you will learn about problems from both sides and hopefully, how to deal with them in a practical sense. But make no mistake, this is a real and legitimate war that we are fighting. In his second letter to the Corinthian church, the Apostle Paul writes, "For the weapons of our warfare are not of the flesh but have divine power to destroy strongholds. We destroy argument and every lofty opinion raised against the knowledge of God, and take every thought captive to obey Christ, being ready to punish every disobedience, when your obedience is complete," (2 Cor. 10:4-6). God reminds us through Paul that in the war we fight, we fight with the truth of Scripture and the truth of the life, death, resurrection, and ascension of the Lord Jesus Christ. By this proclamation, we tear down heresies within the church and destroy lofty secular arguments.

It is my deep hope that this book challenges you to examine your own understanding to church history, because as I am fond of saying, it is family history. We are where we are because bold men and women held fast to the truth of the Word of God, combating all that does not submit to that Final Authority.

CHAPTER 1

ESTABLISHING THE NEW TESTAMENT CANON

"There are some things in them that are hard to understand, which the ignorant and unstable twist to their own destruction, as they do the other Scriptures."
2 Peter 3:16

It seems that in each generation of believers there is one major issue about the Christian faith that must be worked through or defended. Whether this is defending the faith against the Gnostics, the Arian heresy, the disputes between Calvin and Arminius, the rise of Liberalism, or postmodernism, Christians have been called to stay true to the truth revealed in Scripture. This is even documented in the early church as documented in the Book of Acts. Acts 15 deals extensively with how Jewish-cultured Christians were to interact with the Gentile-cultured Christians (Acts 15:1-21). The set the Christian precedent for how major doctrinal problems were to be handled. Councils were called, synods held, and the issues were hammered out by many who followed the Lord Jesus. But within the first few centuries of the Church, writing of the Gospels and Epistles along with anti-Christian writings were being circulated throughout the Roman Empire. As a result, many believers started to call for an understanding of what would be accepted as Scripture.

So, what were the reasons for organizing the canon of New Testament Scripture? Why were some books accepted as God-inspired while others were rejected? Ultimately, who came up with the list of what is now considered the 27 books of the New Testament? This opening chapter seeks to answer such questions.

To begin our discussion, we must first understand what was already considered Scripture during the foundation of the Church while Apostles like Peter and Paul were preaching, and what continued to be accepted as Scripture long after their deaths. According to historian Justo Gonzalez, "There was no question, except among Gnostics and Marcionites, that the Hebrew Scriptures were part of the Christian canon. This was important as proof that God had been preparing the way for the advent of Christianity."[1] This is made clearer as one looks to the pages of Scripture itself. The Apostle Paul repeatedly refers to the Hebrew Scriptures to assist his instruction to believers around the world (see Rom. 3:4, 10-18; 1 Cor. 2:16; Eph. 4:26). Likewise James (James 2:11), Peter (1 Pet. 3:12, 14), the author of Hebrews (Heb. 1:5-9, 12), and John (Rev. 14:14) all continue to show

---

[1] Justo Gonzalez, *The Story of Christianity, Volume 1: The Early Church to the Dawn of the Reformation* (New York City, NY: HarperOne, 2010), 75.

the wide acceptance of the Hebrew Scriptures as authoritative in the context of the fulfillment that Jesus Himself brought during his time on earth.

With the issue well documented that the leaders of the immediate post-Ascension church continued to use Hebrew Scripture as a legitimate form of holy text, we must now turn to answer the question about the New Testament writings. What was it about these writings in particular that so segregated from the rest of texts written during that time to be considered Scripture? Furthermore, when we read the words of Peter, Peter is already calling Paul's work Scripture. "He writes the same way in all his letters, speaking in them of these matters. His letters contain some things that are hard to understand, which ignorant and unstable people distort, *as they do the other Scriptures*, to their own destruction," (2 Pet. 3:16, emphasis added). However, before we can address the New Testament canon in the positive, we must first address the canon in light of the negative.

Let us begin with an interesting subject, namely a man called Marcion. With varied opinions on him, he was eventually condemned a heretic[2], Marcion was a proponent of organizing first century Christian writings into a canon of Scripture.[3] In fact, Jefford states of the author whom he is

---

[2] E. Ferguson, *Evangelical Dictionary of Theology: Second Edition*, ed. Walter A. Elwell (Grand Rapids, MI: Baker Academic, 2001), 735.

[3] Clayton N. Jefford, "The First New Testament: Marcion's Scriptural Canon by Jason BeDuhn (A Review)." *Journal of Early Christian Studies* 22, no. 3 (Fall 2014) 471-472.

reviewing, "[He] is less attracted to Marcion himself and more to the influence on the development of the Christian canon, stating from the outset that we, 'know the name of the individual responsible for the first New Testament.'"[4] While Marcion may have contributed to the organization of a compilation of manuscripts considered to be the "first New Testament," many like Ferguson do not give him such credence, as his compilation was filled with Gnosticism and heavily edited portions of Luke and other Epistles. This in turn led to a sped up "formulation of the orthodox canon, creed, and organization of the church."[5]

With the rejection of Marcion's New Testament, we need to understand a better definition of what would be considered appropriate for canonical use. It should be understood that the New Testament canon was determined firstly and superintedently by God. Secondly, it was determined by what the early church had already accepted as traditional and liturgical. Therefore, the canon was determined by the approval of the church and was demonstrated in the lists of the church fathers and councils.

Perhaps some words from Gonzalez will help our understanding:

> It is important to realize that in the first four or five centuries of Christianity there were dozens—perhaps hundreds, most of the now lost—of Gospels and writings about the acts of Mary and the

---

[4] Ibid., 471.

[5] Ferguson, *Evangelical Dictionary*, 735.

apostles. It is not true, however, that such writings were trying to find their way into the canon, and that the church suppressed some of them. The truth is that the non-canonical Gospels fall into two categories. Some of them, dating mostly from the second century—with the possible exception of the *Gospel of Thomas*, some of whose material may have been earlier—are Gnostic Gospels. Each of these was considered scripture by a particular group which rejected all others, and therefore had no interest in including their book in the nascent canon of the New Testament. They were never considered part of a canon either by the orthodox Christian community —which rejected them—or by their own proponents —who rejected the notion that there could be more than one inspired Gospel. The second category, mostly dating from the third century of later, includes pious stories about Jesus. The church never rejected these. It simply did not include them in the canon—the list of sacred books—of the New Testament. They continued to be read, with little opposition, for centuries, and it is not uncommon to find in medieval cathedrals depictions of episodes taken from such documents. One example of many is the *Protoevangelium of James*, which tells the story of Mary's parents, Anna and Joachim—a story that came to be an accepted part of the Christian tradition, and which is often found in medieval art and literature.

Next to the Gospels, the book of Acts and the

Pauline Epistles enjoyed early recognition. Thus, by the end of the second century the core of the canon was established: the four Gospels, Acts, and the Pauline Epistles. On the shorter books that appear toward the end of the present canon, there was no consensus until a much later date; but there was also little debate. The book of Revelation, widely accepted by the third century, was questioned after the conversion of Constantine, for its words about the prevailing culture and the empire seemed too harsh. It was in the second half of the fourth century that a complete consensus was achieved regarding exactly which books ought to be included in the New Testament, and which ought not to be included.[6]

One of the fascinating things that Gonzalez brings up are these ideas of acceptance and consensus. In many of the documents I have read, these ideas are never presented against any sort of standard. That is, by what standard are we measuring acceptance and consensus? While we do not have the time to examine these further, it is worth noting that this cannot mean acceptance by only the Christian populous.

While all of this helps the believer understand what books were now officially considered Scripture as well as when that took place, the key question becomes, "How?" How did those church leaders at the various councils (the

---

[6] Gonzalez, *The Early Church*, 76-77.

Council of Carthage in particular) determine to accept the Gospel of Matthew or Luke over the Gospel of Thomas. Peckham's work is particularly helpful when attempting to show the how. Without attempting to rewrite his entire defense, these deciding factors can be broken down into smaller, easier to understand chunks. First, Peckham points out that in order for a Gospel-era book or Apostle-era letter to be considered, it must contain what he calls, "Propheticity and Apolstolicity."[7] What this really means is that the works that would be considered must exhibit some kind of proof that a writer had divine authority *and* a divine commission.[8]

Practically speaking, this gives us a better understanding as to why only two of Paul's four letters to the Corinthians were included in the canon. Paul gives us proof of these other letters in 1 Corinthians 5:9 and 2 Corinthians 3-4. Our conclusion must be that these letters were by Paul and from Paul, not by Paul from God.

The second criteria that must be met is what Peckham calls, "Antiquity," meaning, "the contemporaries of Jesus Christ had to be alive when the books were written, otherwise the witness would not be apostolic."[9]

The third accepted criteria Peckham calls, "Consistency, Congruity, and Continuity."[10] Essentially, this third requirement forces us to answer the question, "Does

---

[7] Peckham, 240.

[8] Ibid., 240.

[9] Ibid., 242.

[10] Ibid.

what *is* written match what *was* written?" Put another way, "New light from God will not contradict old light (Deut. 13:1-3; Mal. 3:6; Isa. 8:20; Matt. 5:17-18, 24:35)."[11]

Finally, Peckham argues that in order for Scripture to be acceptable, it must have "Self-Authentication by Divine Purpose."[12] What he goes on to explain is that there must be some sort of proof or evidence that what was written was God-inspired or God-breathed. This is a slight and subtle difference from his first requirement, but it is still a stark difference. To put it plainly, someone might be charged to deliver a message from God, but in and of itself does not make it divine Scripture. For example, certain men are called to preach God's divine Word, but the words they speak during the course of the sermon are not all inspired and to be taken as Scripture.

Therefore, the conclusion that Peckham reaches is that in order for something to be held acceptable as a part of the New Testament Canon, it must fit into each of these four categories. These categories, then, help build a fence around what believers consider to be their immovable and closed canon of holy writ. The fence keeps in what meets this set of requirements and at the same locks out anything that may be masquerading as something that looks like it might fit. Ultimately, the establishment of the New Testament was no easy task.

In his article on the entirety of the Bible Canon, J. R. McRay reminds us, "The formation of the NT must,

---

[11] Ibid., 243.

[12] Ibid.

therefore, be regarded as a process rather than an event, and a historical rather than a biblical matter."[13] What is important for the believer to understand is that this process was not flippant.

From the time of Christ until around A. D. 397, men and women were writing what they thought God was showing them, and pastors were doing their best to discern what to teach to their respective flocks. Also during this time, they fought off governmental persecution, neighborly persecution, and heretical teaching brought on by those who hate God. Yet, through all of this, the Divine Hand of Providence preserved, protected, and guided all that would bring him most glory.

---

[13] J. R. McRay, *Evangelical Dictionary*, 156.

CHAPTER 2

ON PELAGIANISM AND AUGUSTINE

"Therefore, just as sin came into the world through one man, and death through sin, and so death spread to all men because all sinned." Romans 5:12

Throughout the course of church history, there have been major and minor conflicts and disagreements about what the Scriptures teach and what believers ought to do in light of its commands. In the Gospels, we see Jesus rightly teaching his followers and opponents what the Torah actually said. In Acts and the Epistles, we see the Apostles teaching against heresy from the Judaizers and pre-Gnostics, as well as teaching sound doctrine. This very pattern continued into the age of the early church fathers among men like Augustine, Jerome, Pelagius, and others. After the Apostles had left the scene, the church continued to face theological opposition and was forced to deliver sound, biblical answers in response. However, as soon as some issues were solidified by the teachings at various councils and synods, more problems inevitably arose. One particular heresy was brought to the forefront of the Christian world by a man named Pelagius, whose teaching has come to bear his name. In this chapter, we will see the history surrounding the Pelagian controversy, namely between Pelagius and Augustine, including its roots, growth, and its eventual condemnation. To do this, the chapter will be broken into three parts: (1) The history of Pelagius and his thoughts on man's sin nature; (2) The growth in popularity of Pelagianism; and (3) Augustine's response and condemnation of Pelagius.

History of Pelagius

Pelagius was born in Britain circa A. D. 350 to Christian parents—his father a physician and his mother a Celt—both of whom had great ambitions for their son. This becomes evident when we see that history records that Pelagius was given "a good background in the classics and the earlier Church Fathers, [and] was especially well grounded in the Scriptures."[14] While Ferguson states that Pelagius was "well grounded" in the Scriptures, it seems more likely that he was instead well familiar with them. For, while he was able to discern various orthodox Christian doctrines, Ferguson notes that Pelagius saw in Scripture, "ideas such as free will, moral conduct, doing the will of the Father, good works, following the example of Jesus Christ, and a system of rewards and punishment."[15] History further

---

[14] Everett Ferguson, *Church History: The Rise and Growth of the Church in Its Cultural, Intellectual, and Political Context*, 2nd ed., Vol. 1 (Grand Rapids, MI: Zondervan, 2013), 279.

[15] Ibid., 280.

reports that in addition to his classical education, he "gave himself much to the study of the Greek church writers."[16]

Therefore, as he developed his theology, Pelagius pursued a Christian version of humanistic-moralism. That is, because of the serious questions he raised regarding free will, original sin, grace, and predestination, he came to some very unorthodox answers. In fact, Bruce Shelley has defined his beliefs this way, "Pelagianism is that teaching… which stresses one's ability to take the initial steps toward salvation by one's own efforts, apart from special grace."[17] This is a dramatic departure from traditional Christian doctrine. Men like the Paul, James, and Peter make it abundantly clear that man cannot come to God on his own terms, much less by his own strength.

However, Pelagius began to develop what can only be described as some sort of middle ground between what is now known as Augustinianism and Arianism or Manichaeanism. Despite his critique against Arianism, Ferguson notes that in reality Pelagianism is "akin to the Arian controversy in that both had a soteriological interest—Arianism from the divine side and Pelagianism from the human viewpoint."[18]

Furthermore, and consistent with his monastic and

---

[16] Philip Schaff, "The Pelagian Controversy—A Historical Essay," *Bibliotheca Sacra* 5, no. 18 (May 1848), 205.

[17] Bruce Shelley, "Pelagius, Pelagianism," *Evangelical Dictionary of Theology*, 2nd ed., Walter A. Elwell, ed. (Grand Rapids, MI: Baker Academic, 2001), 897.

[18] Ferguson, *Church History*, 276.

ascetic approach to life as a believer, Pelagius was certain that his efforts of apparent godliness would secure for him the salvation he so desired. Schaff notes that this kind of morality "rests mainly in externals,"[19] and that as a result of his full confidence in himself as opposed to confidence in God, Pelagius "had the monkish imagination that man is able, in pursuit of perfection, (an object within his reach even in this world,) to go beyond what the law requires at his hands."[20] And, as we can certainly see, this reliance on self for complete obedience to the law, coupled with the belief that earthly perfection is actually attainable, became the breeding ground for two things: (1) Fierce opposition from orthodox men like Augustine, and (2) Support for and mutation of the heresy by equally zealous men like Coelestius.

Our question now becomes: How did Pelagius come to these conclusions? That is, if it is true that man can attain enough righteousness to merit his salvation, as well as attain earthly perfection so there is no need for sanctification, how was he able to defend these positions? What evidence from Scripture was he using to support these ideas whereby he was able to gain a large following from this unorthodox teaching? The answers to these questions center around how Pelagius viewed the doctrines of Original Sin and Freedom of the Will.

Here, it is worth noting that the traditional, orthodox definitions of both terms. For in order to see what has been

---

[19] Schaff, "The Pelagian Controversy," 207.

[20] Ibid., 207-208.

established against what Pelagius concluded, will only set the realities of their differences in plain view. For Augustine, in his work, *Ad Simplicianum*, it was explicit that original sin is "the belief that in Adam all his progeny also sinned and were punished with physical death, evil inclinations, and (most controversially) guilt."[21] With this comprehensive definition of Original Sin, it naturally follows that the Freedom of the Will of man is damaged beyond repair by anyone or anything other than a divine source.

It is here that we must turn our attention to what some have called the subjective aspects of these doctrines. Quoting Benjamin Warfield, Schaff writes:

> The chief controversies of the first four centuries and the resulting definitions of doctrine, concerned the nature of God and the person of Christ; and it was not until these theological and Christological questions were well upon their way to final settlement, that the Church could turn its attention to the more subjective side of truth. Meanwhile she bore in her bosom a full recognition, side by side, of the freedom of the will, the evil consequences of the

---

[21] Eugene Teselle, "The Background: Augustine and the Pelagian Controversy," *Grace for Grace: The Debates After Augustine and Pelagius*, Alexander Y. Hwang, Brian J. Matz, and Augustine Casiday, eds. (Washington, D. C.: The Catholic University of America Press, 2014), 9.

fall, and the necessity of grace for salvation.[22]

This relates to an earlier statement where the subjectiveness of the Christian faith played a crucial role in the fifth century. There were objective truths clearly laid out in Scripture that the early Church Fathers had to settle before any less explicit doctrine of faith could be addressed.

As a result, Pelagius disagreed with the established creeds that the sin of Adam was inherited by the whole of the human race thereafter. In some ways, it is like the modern psychological argument of *tabula rasa*, or that people are born with a morally blank slate. This goes with his assertion that men had the ability to freely choose to do either good or evil. In fact, in his book, *The Doctrines That Divide*, Erwin Lutzer writes, "To quote Pelagius, man has 'the absolutely equal ability at every moment to do good or evil.' Therefore, man can, if he so wishes, live sinlessly."[23] Clearly this begs the question: If this is true, who wouldn't want to live sinlessly?

Further, Teselle writes that while Pelagius was indeed serious about sin, he was not convinced that sin could be imputed to progeny or that a wrong choice could change the

---

[22] Benjamin Warfield, "Introductory Essay on Augustin and the Pelagian Controversy," *Nicene and Post-Nicene Fathers*, Series 1, Vol. 5, Philip Schaff, ed. (Grand Rapids, MI: Christian Classics Ethereal Library, 2020), 12.

[23] Erwin Lutzer, *The Doctrines That Divide: A Fresh Look at the Historic Doctrines That Separate Christians* (Grand Rapids, MI: Kregel Publications, 1998), 155.

inherent good nature of man.[24]

Growth in Popularity

With Original Sin dismissed and the Freedom of the Will placed squarely as the root desire of man, there would inevitably be those who took the teachings of Pelagius even further. One such man was Coelestius. Coelestius was a student of Pelagius during his tenure in Rome. In an attempt to flee raids on the city, the two of them set out for Africa in 411, "whence Pelagius son afterwards departed for Palestine, leaving the bolder and more contentious Coelestius at Carthage."[25]

However, despite this uncanny ability to be contentious, Coelestius was able to amass for himself quite the following. Schaff writes that he was able to do this because of his "talents and his ascetic zeal."[26] What his talents were are not made clear by Schaff. Perhaps it was elegance of speech. Perhaps it was his emphatic displays of asceticism and apparent contrition. Regardless, many began to listen to what he had to say. Furthermore, he took the basic ideas of Pelagius—no Original Sin, total Freedom of the Will, the ability to achieve salvation apart from grace—and developed them into seven distinct arguments.

Schaff writes that at a council in 412, Coelestius was charged with the following errors:

------

[24] Teselle, *Grace for Grace*, 4.

[25] Warfield, *Fathers*, 19.

[26] Schaff, "The Pelagian Controversy," 212.

1. Adam was created mortal, and would have died even if he had not sinner. 2. Adam's sin injured himself only, and not the human race. 3. Children come into the world in the same state in which Adam was before his fall. 4. Neither does the whole human race die in consequence of Adam's fall, nor the whole human race rise again in consequence of Christ's resurrection. 5. Even unbaptized children are saved. 6. The law leads into the kingdom of heaven, in the same way with the gospel. 7. Even before the coming of Christ, there were men without sin.[27]

All of these points of teaching eventually fell under the heading of Pelagianism. This, despite the fact that at the time, Pelagius himself was living and teaching in Palestine. Further, at that same council, Coelestius was condemned as a heretic by men like Paulinus and Bishop Aurelius, "and refused to reject any of the propositions charged against him."[28]

The Response of Augustine and the Church

As a contemporary of Pelagius, why has Saint Augustine not engaged thus far? Clearly he was an active teacher, communicator, writer, and traveler for the church; so why does it seem at this point that he was not fighting against such rampant and obvious heresy? While indeed it is

---

[27] Ibid.

[28] Warfield, *Fathers*, 19-20.

true that Augustine was not immediate to counter the arguments brought forth under the claims of Pelagianism, we should not take his silence as inaction. Rather, Augustine was calculated in his approach to these teachings and in his responses. Furthermore, it must be noted that the church catholic responded to the claims of Pelagianism fiercely. That is, we must not think that Augustine was the only bastion of church purity and integrity.

One of the reasons for Augustine's apparent initial silence had more to do with the technology of the as opposed to a supposed lack of interest. Commenting on this delayed response, Teselle writes, "For several years, Augustine was reluctant to attack Pelagius; partly because of his influential friends, partly because it was difficult to get copies of his writings. There was only a 'theologians' quarrel' between them."[29] What he means here is that Augustine was not going to blindly attack someone under the mere suspicions or claims of heresy without first knowing that a particular heresy was being actively promoted.

However, when Augustine had been fully briefed on the teachings of Pelagianism—including the teachings of Pelagius and Coelestius, respectively—he did not remain quiet. In fact, Augustine led a systematic defense of the true Gospel and succinctly dismantled this new unorthodox doctrine. For our purposes here, there is only space for a brief examination of Augustine's rebuttals due in large part to the extensive nature of his arguments. In examining the

---

[29] Teselle, *Grace for Grace*, 5.

doctrine of Original Sin, Augustine first considered that which came before, namely the "primitive state of man," or the nature of man before the Fall. Schaff writes, "The primitive state of man included in itself the possibility of sin, and this formed the imperfection of that state."[30] This means that Adam was not simply a blank slate with the ability to choose the good or the evil. Rather, Adam lived in an untested, imperfect state that included both the possibility to sin and the possibility not to sin. This goes far beyond a simple choice. Furthermore, the sin that caused the Fall was more than just the physical eating of the forbidden fruit, but that which caused the eating of the fruit; namely a wicked desire to be like God.

Schaff, annotating the words of Augustine writes:

> The sin of Adam consisted not essentially in partaking of the fruit, for this in itself was neither evil nor hurtful, but in *disobedience* to the commandment of God. "Obedience was enjoined in that command, as the virtue which is for the rational creature the *mother*, as it were, and *guardian* of all virtues." The principle or root of sin, on the contrary was *pride, self-seeking*, the desire of the will to forsake its source, and to become a source for itself.[31]

Therefore, what Schaff rightly explains is that Augustine looks beyond the mere external action of eating a

---

[30] Schaff, "The Pelagian Controversy," 223.

[31] Ibid., emphasis in original.

piece of fruit. Scripture itself declares that the fruit was both pleasing to the eye and good for food (Gen. 3:6). This inner desire of pride and self-seeking goes far beyond the external morality promoted by Pelagius. For, as noted above, Pelagius could not reconcile how an act of eating could result in the Fall of the entire human race as the entire race had not all eaten the fruit.

Augustine, however, shows that as the federal head of humanity, it was what the breaking of the command supposedly promised that plunged the world into chaos. Schaff says that Augustine "passes from the appearance to the substance, from the surface into the deep. He stops not with the outward act, but fastens his eye first of all on the inward mind that lies at the ground of all actions."[32] This means that as inward disobedience to the commands of God lead to outward action of disobedience, this also has a devastating effect on the Will of Man. In fact, these effects are so severe that Schaff summarizes Augustine's view of the consequence involve a loss of freedom, where, "The will, which with supporting grace would have become a fountain of good, was turned, by forsaking God, into a fountain of sin;"[33] a darkening in understanding;[34] a loss of the grace of God;[35] the loss of the Edenic paradise;[36] and arguably most

---

[32] Ibid., 224.

[33] Ibid.

[34] Ibid.

[35] Ibid.

[36] Ibid.

burdensome, "concupiscence, or the lusting of the flesh against the spirit."[37]

The final discovery noted by Augustine is both in direct accordance with the Scriptures and in direct opposition to Pelagianism. That is, now with an indwelt sin nature, man lusts for more of that which condemned him in the first place. Therefore, Augustine shows that not only is Original Sin a true and legitimate problem for humanity, he also shows that there are at least two pressing results that Pelagius taught against; namely a loss of the Freedom of the Will and a need for Divine Grace. That is to say that in a fallen state, both for Adam and the rest of humanity, Augustine shows that sin breaks the Will of Man to go good and his desire turns to a craving for evil. Further, since man can now only crave to do that which is evil, he cannot choose to bring himself under his own power to a right standing with God. Instead, he *must* rely solely on the grace of God.

The response from the church catholic was similar at the Council of Carthage in 418. In fact, Ferguson records that the council approved nine canons, six of which were used in the condemnation of Pelagianism. Ferguson writes that three of those were "on original sin, pronouncing anathema on those who say death is not the result of Adam's sin."[38] Another three "were on grace, anathematizing those who say grace only brings a remission of past sins, those who say grace aids us not in understanding... and those who say

---

[37] Ibid.

[38] Ferguson, *Church History*, 281.

grace only enables us to do more easily what we do."[39] The final three canons settled an ecclesiastical issue regarding passages like 1 John 1:8 and the Lord's Prayer.[40] After the Council, Pelagius and his followers were banished by the emperor, and a man named Zosimus excommunicated Pelagius and Coelestius from the church.[41] Finally, in the year 431, almost twenty years after the heresy rose to the surface, Pelagius, Coelestius, and others were fully and finally deposed by Pope Celestine at the Council of Ephesus.[42]

Conclusion

If the history of the church has shown us anything, it has shown us that there will always be disagreements among fellow believers. The problem comes when these disagreements go unchecked against the authority of Scripture. The heresy of Pelagianism is no different. Pelagius, as noted, was well familiar with the content of Scripture. However, he was lacking in his understanding of the overall context. As a result, he began to develop a theology that was truly anthropocentric, wherein he worked to make man the chief of his own salvation. He posited that certainly only one man can be responsible for his own actions. He could not reconcile in his mind the concept of the

---

[39] Ibid.

[40] Ibid.

[41] Ibid.

[42] Ibid., 282.

sin of one man and the imputation of sin to others. This thinking leads to a defective Christology. That is, if sin cannot be imputed to the human race by one disobedient action, then certainly righteousness cannot be imputed to those who have turned their face toward God in repentance, drawn by the Holy Spirit.

Augustine methodically worked to argue against the claims of Pelagius and his more even more zealous followers. He shows in his works and from the Scriptures that man has been ruined from the Fall. He shows that man cannot achieve his own righteousness by following the Law —a point that, again, Scripture makes clear. In short, the response that Augustine gave to Pelagius and to the rest of the church is one of traditional, orthodox Christianity. It is in line with what Scripture teaches from beginning to end. Lastly, while Pelagius, his followers, and his ideas fell away from the main stage of church history, there are still remnants of this ideology left lingering in the contemporary church.

CHAPTER 3

THE RISE OF THE PAPACY

Be an anti-papist.

Historically, many questions arise about the origins of certain practices in Christianity, including the origins of creeds, adherence of major doctrinal issues, the style and flow of modern worship services, and the like. One great question with regard to the church as an organization revolves around the ideal of papal authority and a centralized church headquarters. For this particular discussion, the following must be asked: Why did Rome become the central hub of Christian power and leadership? What was the cause of this? And, who were some of the leaders that supported this idea? Approaching this topic is no small feat, as this aspect of church history spans hundreds of years' worth of events leading up to this decision and its overall results for many years after.

To begin, while no clear defining date has ever been established for the rise of the papacy in Rome, some attribute its early beginnings to the Apostle Peter upon his visit to Rome.[43] Some also argue that it is possible that Rome originally might have started out as a "group of bishops who jointly led the church."[44] While it is obvious that none of these claims can be substantiated beyond speculation, no matter how educated the speculation may be, one thing is certain: A singular leader for the visible church body, or at least the desire to have such a leader can be traced to biblical precedent.

Starting as far back as the accounts in Genesis, we see that singular leaders appear, as appointed by God, to lead His people throughout the course of history.[45] Genesis 12 speaks of the call of Abram; the call and rise of Joseph (culminating in Gen. 41); Moses leading Israel out of Egypt in Exodus, and countless other examples throughout the Old Testament. The pattern continues in type in the New Testament with leaders such as the Apostles Peter, James, John, Paul, and Jude, who all become major figureheads in the history of the church. Many often recall the words of Jesus to Peter in Matthew 16, "And I tell you that you are Peter, and on this rock I will build my church, and the gates

---

[43] Gonzalez, *The Early Church*, 282.

[44] Ibid.

[45] It should be noted here on the outset that this is where the idea for the papacy takes a wrong turn in that these leaders were all type and shadow of the Leader to come, who is Christ. More could be said about this, but suffice to say for now, in the scope of our discussion, that those in support of the papacy miss this point.

of Hades will not overcome it," (Matt. 16:18).

In all this, we can see that one leader usually emerges that many look to for wisdom and guidance as they try to live out practically what has been communicated, either by what has been preached or what has been written down. With the precedent set, we must now look at how this great change came about. Prior to the papacy, Christians—with the exception of a few—seemed to live fameless lives persevering through the different reigns of terror brought by the Roman government. As the centuries wore on, the Roman Empire was constantly being harassed by the Germanic tribes from the North. Interestingly, one scholar, Guy Halsall, shares that this Germanic harassment was, indeed, no harassment at all. Coming from the vantage point of "the winners write history," Halsall asks if the "German barbarians" were really all that barbaric. He says, "Few people have expressed the preconception as clearly as did Henri Pirenne: the barbarians were irresistibly drawn towards the Mediterranean, 'happy regions where the mildness of the climate and the fertility of the soil were matched by the charms and the wealth of civilization.'"[46] Furthermore, Halsall asserts that "the traditional assumption of a natural barbarian desire to conquer the Roman Empire lacks any empirical foundation."[47]

While Halsall may be asserting these things, the

---

[46] Guy Halsall, "Two Worlds Become One: A 'Counter-Intuitive' View of the Roman Empire and 'Germanic' Migration," *German History*, 32 no. 4, 522.

[47] Ibid.

opposite of his claims remain just as valid; that is, the idea that all the Germanic tribes wanted to do was learn to be civilized and relax by the beach also lacks any empirical foundation. According to Gonzalez, it is because of the weakening of the Western Roman Empire that the Germanic tribes were able to commander or conquer some of the Roman land and, "Thus, the most prestigious bishop in the West, that of Rome, became the focal point for regaining a unity that had been shattered by the invasion."[48]

Out of this necessity for unity, a man called Leo the Great came into great focus during this time. In fact, C. T. Marshall writes:

> Leo I was a great administrator who sought to control all of Christendom. The chaos left by invading barbarians, especially the Vandals and Huns, made local churches turn to Rome for help and advice. Leo made significant inroads into imperial power in the West, even to assuming the old imperial title Pontifex Maximus (chief priest), which the emperors had dropped.[49]

It is at this early stage in the development of the papacy that one can start to see that not only would the pope begin to play a part in the role of spiritual leadership, but political leadership as well. For instance, it is well documented that Leo the Great served as a sort of mediator

---

[48] Gonzalez, *The Early Church*, 282.

[49] C. T. Marshall, *Evangelical Dictionary*, 680.

who was able to confront great political conflict with—what appeared to be—ease. Marshall relates the story of how Attila the Hun came to invade Rome and Leo was the one who came out to meet him and convinced him to turn back, and Attila did just that and died shortly thereafter.[50]

It seems, therefore, that the position of the pope became increasingly beneficial, not just for its religious purposes, but even more so for its political purposes. To bring this to a further point of clarity, we only need to look to the third and fourth centuries where we see great leaders with a heavier emphasis on church leadership rather than political: Athanasius, Jerome, Augustine of Hippo, and John Chrysostom to name a few.[51] Many of these men lived monastic lives in which they fought for the preservation of the Holy Scriptures of the Christian faith. The key issues for these men were issues of doctrine; specifically revolving around the two natures of Jesus.

After Leo, there is a long succession of the popes of Rome that essentially became the puppets of the Western Roman Empire. According to Gonzalez, many of the Roman leaders—especially those in the West—"demanded that the popes support their theological positions. Those who refused were treated harshly."[52] It is in this interesting circle of affirmation between the rulers of Rome and the "rulers" of the church that we find a most curious situation.

---

[50] Ibid.

[51] Gonzalez, *The Early Church*, 199-252.

[52] Ibid., 289.

According to Gonzalez[53] and Harting, even though the idea of the pope was supposed to be based on the direct successors of the Apostle Peter, history seems to play out that the rulers designated who they wish to see as bishop—while taking the title of pope—and in return the popes would crown or anoint the new ruler of the empire.[54]

We may be able to see the strengths of having a centralized body or leader in an empire such as the Roman Empire, but we must also consider some of the drawbacks of having such power being granted to a singular church leader. One of the major setbacks to having a singular human leader during the time of the early church, but more specifically up until the Reformation, is the idea that a person could be considered the final source of authority over and against Scripture. For instance, when we look at the abuse of the papal leadership which led up to the Reformation, Martin Luther relentlessly attacked church leadership against a myriad of problems. In his article discussing the matter of indulgences, McNally quotes Luther as saying:

> When many people from Wittenberg ran after indulgences to Juterbog and Zerbst, I did not yet know—as surely as my Lord Christ has redeemed me—what indulgences were, but no one else knew

---

[53] Ibid., 283-285, 323.

[54] Henry Mayr-Harting, "Charlemagne, the Saxons, and the Imperial Coronation of 800," *The English Historical Review* 111, no. 444 (Nov. 1996), 1113-1133.

either. I carefully began to preach that one could do something better and more certain than to purchase indulgences.[55]

Furthermore, the average believer of the time was being restricted on what they could learn and understand, having to rely solely upon the teachings of the priest or pope. These things, along with many others, including having to confess one's sins to the local parish priest—a clear misunderstanding of 1 Timothy 2:5—took power originally granted to church leadership to shepherd Christ's flock, and turned it into something that it was never intended to be. This was especially problematic under the reign of Charlemagne and the kings following him, where priests and bishops were becoming wealthy landowners. Gonzalez says:

> The church was also affected. Since bishoprics and abbeys often had vast holdings of land, bishops, abbots and abbesses became magnates whose support everyone sought. Therefore, the question of who possessed the authority to name those who would fill such positions [as in one who would become the next bishopric, abbot, etc.] became one of enormous political significance.[56]

---

[55] Robert E. McNally, S. J., "The Ninety-Five Theses of Martin Luther: 1517-1967," *Theological Studies*, 28 no. 3 (Sept. 1967), 450.

[56] Gonzalez, *The Early Church*, 318.

In short, the rise of the papacy in Rome was primarily the result of the invading Germanic tribes from the North, which over time slowly wore down the weakening Western Roman Empire. The Roman papacy continued to dominate throughout church history up until the dawn of the Reformation in large part due to the royal and religious—that is, impersonal and political—sway the papacy developed with both the emperors and the people. And finally, the positive side to this agreement among those in the Empire was that of political civility—as in the case with Leo the Great and the Vandals and the Huns—as well as theological acuity. The negative results came in the form of an overbearing attitude of religiosity, where it seemed that people had to not only work out their salvation (Phil. 2:12), but also had to work *for* their salvation. The latter of which the Lord Jesus has already completed for the believer.

CHAPTER 4

EARLY REFORMERS WYCLIFFE AND HUSS

"Today you will cook a goose, but 100 years from now you will have a swan which you can neither roast or boil!" - John Huss

So far in our overview of church history, the wars have raged primarily within the confines of the Christian brotherhood. Now, we see the war begins to be fought outside the true Christian church and an apostate church. Our focus here turns to two key figures that were apart of what some might call the early Reformation. Often when the Reformation is discussed, the first names that come to mind are John Calvin and Marin Luther, and for anyone with my kind of Christian upbringing, that's the extent of the knowledge of the Reformation. However, there were many other influential Christian leaders, and for our focus here, namely John Wycliffe and John Huss. These men carried with them prolific ideas that related to the everyday working out of the Christian faith that influenced, and continues to influence, many who follow the Lord Jesus.

Depending on which of these individuals you end up studying, you will find yourself in one of two camps for each man. For Wycliffe, the camp you will most likely end up in is that of the understanding it as a familiar name closely associated with a Christian organization or book publisher. The other prominent camp you would take up citizenship would be that of total unrecognition. The latter of the two camps is most likely the primary camp for Huss. This is, of course, understandable given that within the context of the history of the church, many names and events are given more prominence and prestige than others.

The 95 Theses of Martin Luther, the strong and well-articulated beliefs of John Calvin, the heroism of Joan of Arc, are all historical giants, and not just in the realm of the church.

For our purposes here, the focus on Wycliffe and Huss will help us see the impact that these two "pre-Reformers" had on those that would soon follow. Their lives, beliefs, and deaths had profound meanings on the lives of those later in church history. With this in mind, let us turn to the life of John Wycliffe.

Wycliffe was born circa 1330[57] in a small Yorkshire village, Wycliffe-on-Tees.[58] Although his family owned land, Wycliffe seemed to live in a general sense of obscurity with very little known about his young life. What is key, however, is the fact that he was a very learned individual, who at the age of twelve was attending Oxford University where he

---

[57] R. G. Clouse, *Evangelical Dictionary*, 1304.

[58] Gonzalez, *The Early Church*, 412.

was, "A brilliant scholar who mastered the late medieval scholastic tradition, [and] came to the attention of the government."[59] While his political life and interests serve a purpose for study, our focus needs to remain on the fact that it was during his time at Oxford that he developed his "unorthodox" approach to getting Scripture into the hands of the people.

Interestingly, as a result of the changing political climate, in what is now modern day Great Britain, "A series of English statutes (1351, 1353, 1363) sought to limit papal influence, first by making election to ecclesiastical positions independent of the pope, and then by forbidding appeals to courts outside of England."[60] These statutes, which helped curb an ever-growing presence of strength in the papacy, were crucial to the acceptance of the teachings of Wycliffe during that time.

While speaking and teaching, Wycliffe is known for his many essays about the Christian faith and how it pertained to everyday living. His key work was published in 1376, entitled, *On Civil Dominion*. This work asserted that only those who are in right standing with God should be able to hold political authority.[61] Additionally, Wycliffe indicates in this work that:

The Gospel alone is sufficient to rule the lives of

---

[59] Clouse, *Evangelical Dictionary*, 1304.

[60] Gonzalez, *The Early Church*, 412.

[61] Clouse, *Evangelical Dictionary*, 1305.

Christians everywhere… any additional rules made to govern men's conduct added nothing to the perfection already found in the Gospel of Jesus Christ… no high-ranking clergy should have prisons to punish transgressors.[62]

This extreme view took on extraordinary criticism, such that he was repeatedly confronted by the hierarchy of the church,[63] while those same people in positions of authority were clamoring for his teaching position he held at Oxford.[64] Despite all of these challenges, Wycliffe did not and could not back down from his accusers because—as mentioned earlier—these were strongly held, biblically based beliefs. Further, much of what he did is lumped together with the growing legend that he himself translated the Latin Vulgate into English entirely on his own, while possible, is really not probable. But, by his work, he has been dubbed by church history the "Morning Star of the Reformation," largely because of his work of getting the Bible into the common language of his fellow brothers and sisters.

While the road for Wycliffe was certainly troubled, the remainder and end of his life seemed to be almost luxurious compared to that of John Huss. Wycliffe was

---

[62] dcTalk, *Jesus Freaks Vol. II: Stories of Revolutionaries who Changed Their World; Fearing God, Not Man* (Bloomington, MN: Bethany House, 2007), 98.

[63] Ibid.

[64] Clouse, *Evangelical Dictionary*, 1305.

frequently confronted about his positions on Christian doctrine and often asked to reject the content of his own teaching.[65] Firmly refusing to do such a thing, he retired to a small village in Lutterworth, where he suffered two strokes —one fatal—and in 1384, he died. Oddly enough, his story does not end there. Some thirty-one years after his death, the Council of Constance poured over the teachings of Wycliffe and condemned him a heretic. Since he was already dead, "they ordered that his body be dug up, burned, and the ashes scattered in the river. This was finally carried out in 1428. They had hoped that this action would put an end to Wycliffe's teaching and influence, but it did not."[66]

Next, we must examine the contemporary life of the one John Huss, also referred to in various texts as Jan Hus. For our purposes, we will use the former of the two names. Huss was by and large more outspoken than someone like Wycliffe, and as such, used his position in the church to preach hard messages against clerical abuses in the church.[67]

Similar to Wycliffe, Huss's desire to have Scripture available in his native language so greatly motivated him after his appointment to the position of pastor in Prague's Bethlehem chapel that he seemed laser focused to that end. For instance:

[Huss's] sermons attacked clerical abuses,

---

[65] Gonzalez, *The Early Church*, 414.

[66] dcTalk, *Jesus Freaks*, 98.

[67] P. Kubright, "Hus, Jan," *Evangelical Dictionary*, 582.

especially the immorality and high living of the clergy… He emphasized the preaching of the Word of God to bring about moral and spiritual change in listeners' lives. To help them read the Scripture, he also revised a Czech translation of the Bible.[68]

However, as one might imagine, preaching vehemently against a religious aristocracy has its problems. One of the issues that brought criticism upon Huss was his accusation against the well-to-do people in the church, calling many of the upper crust leaders "the Lord's fat ones." He also accused them "of fornication, absenteeism, and enriching themselves at the expense of the people."[69]

And what was the reward for such preaching? Huss was hunted down by the pope in order to root out "heresy." After the first failed hunt of getting Huss to recant his sermons, he began attacking almost every area of misdeed in the visible church.

First he declared that an unworthy pope is not to be obeyed… What he questioned was their authority when it was clear that they were acting in their own interests, and not for the welfare of the church. He thus came to the conclusion that the Bible is the final authority by which the pope as well as any Christian

---

[68] Ibid.

[69] Gonzalez, *The Early Church*, 417.

is to be judged.[70]

As these sermons began to circulate, Huss undoubtedly and unapologetically continued to confront the problems he saw within the church. This inevitably led to more individuals in the church aristocracy to call for Huss to either silence himself or to be silenced. After a false promise given to him by the leaders of the Council of Constance, Huss traveled to the meeting place and was immediately "imprisoned and placed on trial for heresy."[71]

As the accusers tried to get Huss to recant his beliefs and his sermons, Huss refused to do so unless they could find something on biblical grounds which would prove his guilt. Unable to find any ground to stake their claim, Huss was sent back to prison for little over a month. Before being taken back to his cell, it is recorded that Huss said, "I appeal to Jesus Christ, the only judge who is almighty and completely just. In his hands I place my cause, since he will judge each, not on the basis of false witnesses and erring councils, but on truth and justice."[72]

Then, a month later, Huss's day of martyrdom arrived. His accusers mocked him, shamed him, and burned him at the stake. Before being burned, they offered him one final chance to recant his strongly held beliefs and teachings. His response was refusal and a prayer, "Lord Jesus, it is for

---

[70] Ibid., 418.

[71] Kubright, *Evangelical Dictionary*, 582.

[72] Gonzalez, *The Early Church*, 419.

thee that I patiently endure this cruel death. I pray thee to have mercy on my enemies."[73]

After understanding the event-filled lives of men like Wycliffe and Huss, one can easily see that their devotion to Jesus was of the utmost priority. Both men faced heavy persecution for their Reformational beliefs that men are accountable to God and God alone for their actions; that the Scripture helps individuals understand that truth; and that people should have access to read and understand Scripture in their own language. Yet, despite the persecution, they held their ground and became stalwart examples of how Christians ought to face opposition to the truth.

---

[73] Ibid.

CHAPTER 5

IN DEFENSE OF THE CHRISTIAN WORLDVIEW AGAINST POSTMODERNISM

Postmodernism is stupid; Stupid is not a good long-term game plan.

In this final chapter, we are going to fast-forward over many interesting years of church history. Many better people have covered the events immediately after Wycliffe and Huss and up closer to the present. However, I want to take time to defend Christianity against postmodernism because this seems to still remain a large problem in the church.

In essence, postmodernism is an attempt to answer the questions that Christianity already answers perfectly well. This is not a new phenomenon as people have always been searching outside of what God has revealed to explain the world around them. Norse, Greek, and Roman mythology all made this attempt. Modern Hinduism with its plethora of deities attempts the same. In all, they reject the true God of the Scriptures, and instead base the characteristics of their gods based on the flawed characteristics of their fellow man.

In short, whether we want to believe it or not, a proper understanding of God has eternal consequences. Therefore, this chapter will demonstrate how the widely accepted view of postmodernism is foolish as it is incoherent and unstable when pressed on the major issues of the day. Postmodernism is crushed under its own weight because of its lack of objectivity. Conversely, the Christian worldview provides a superior set of objective beliefs when considered against ultimate reality, ultimate authority, epistemology, views on mankind, and ultimate morality.

Summary of Postmodernism

As we examine the postmodern worldview, it is of utmost importance that the terms we are using are clearly defined. By the very nature of postmodernism, this is a difficult task for even its most vocal proponent. For example, Amy Orr-Ewing writes, "By its very nature the postmodern worldview is difficult to define, and some would resist calling it such. It is an eclectic movement, originating in aesthetics, architecture, and philosophy."[74] In order to make sense of the lack of clarity provided by postmodernism, James Beilby offers this:

The defining characteristic of *postmodernism* is

---

[74] Amy Orr-Ewing, "Postmodern Challenges to the Bible," in *Beyond Opinion: Living the Faith We Defend*, ed. Ravi Zacharias (Nashville, TN: Thomas Nelson, 2007), 3.

best thought of as a loss of confidence in the modern project and its attempt to formulate perfect, indubitable answers to the questions humans ask. Postmodernism (in its nonrelativistic variety), therefore, does not question the possibility of truth or knowledge. It questions whether our beliefs are absolutely certain whether our descriptions of reality are perfect and exhaustive.[75]

In short, what these authors are attempting to communicate is that the postmodern worldview is attempting to achieve the impossible.

For example, as Beilby points out, the postmodernist is attempting to see if we can be "absolutely certain" about our beliefs, and that that certainty hinges on whether or not one's definitions are "perfect and exhaustive." As a finite being, the postmodernist cannot being to hope to be successful in this endeavor. Put another way, because of his loss of confidence in what he can know or believe, the postmodernist will have to continually redefine his beliefs as the movement progresses, even if that means submitting to absurdity. Therefore, with this working definition, let us dig further into what postmodernism must contend with.

Ultimate Reality

For the postmodernist, the concept of ultimate reality

---

[75] James K. Beilby, *Thinking About Christian Apologetics: What It Is and Why We Do It* (Downers Grove, IL: IVP Academic, 2011), 126.

is either unattainable or it simply cannot exist. That is, when the person of this worldview is lives out his beliefs to their logical ends, he approaches the world with such a great deal of skepticism that there is a complete loss of confidence in the world that surrounds him. This includes his senses, reason, and logic. For example, Douglas Groothuis writes, "Many in the postmodern world have given up on the existence of objective truth entirely and so find no need to pursue it."[76] This rejection of objective truth trickles down into every other aspect of one's system of belief. That is, because nothing can be known to be true, there must be no ultimate reality. Therefore, whatever ultimate claims about reality the postmodernist makes is self-defeating because he has already given up certainty.

Ultimate Authority

Given the above, when the topic of ultimate authority arises, the postmodernist must assume that he is the source of ultimate authority. At its very worst, "postmodernism is a type of relativism."[77] Due to the intensity of relativistic thought, nothing has any sort of fixed meaning. Therefore, the postmodernist is left, by default, being the sole arbiter of what is true concerning everything from language, to

---

[76] Douglas Groothuis, *Christian Apologetics: A Comprehensive Case for Biblical Fatih* (Downers Grove, IL: IVP Academics, 2011), 140.

[77] Glenn B. Siniscalchi, "Postmodernism and the Need for Rational Apologetics in a Post-Conciliar Church," *The Heythrop Journal* 52, no. 5 (Sept. 2011), 751.

morality, and even to human nature.[78]

Epistemology

It is here, the topic of epistemology, where the postmodernist comes to the tipping point of his worldview. In fact, as noted above, since all truth and authority claims are relative, he must take what I'll call an antirealist perspective. On that, James K. Dew and Mark W. Foreman write, "They think it is impossible for a person to view reality as it actually is. For them, all of our perceptions come to us through the subjective filters of our minds. They suggest that truth claims fail to appreciate the various ways our ideas and understanding of reality are shaped and are influenced by the world in which we live. Because of this, they contend absolute truth *does not exist.*"[79]

C. S. Lewis, in his great work, *Mere Christianity*, points out the problem with not being able to know the truth when he discusses the issues of truth and discussing the city of New York. He points out that if there is not objective standard, no one could make the claim that the other was thinking about the real, or true New York and a false one.[80]

What this means then, is that because there is no objective reality and there is no source of ultimate authority

---

[78] Ibid.

[79] James K. Dew and Mark W. Foreman, *How Do We Know? An Introduction to Epistemology* (Downers Grove, IL: IVP Academic, 2014), 50. Emphasis added.

[80] C. S. Lewis, *Mere Christianity* (New York, NY: Collier Books, 1960), 11.

other than himself, only the postmodernist can determine what can be known. However, this also means that in order for any part of his worldview to function, he must either convince others to join him in his absurdity, or he must borrow something that makes sense from the Christian worldview. By making his view function by either of his two options, he immediately negates his position, and has painted himself into a corner he cannot escape.

Mankind

Similar to the myriad of worldviews that are antithetical to Christianity, postmodernism has very little regard for mankind in general and the human being in particular. According to the postmodernist, human beings are simply the product of random chance, their environmental surroundings, cultural influences, and so on. To his view, there is nothing inherently valuable or worthwhile about the individual save for—maybe—the value of personal viability. As such, the only logical conclusion to his argument about the purpose of mankind is that of random chance; fizzing bags of protoplasm. Indeed, it is this lack of value on humanity that moves many in postmodernism into materialism. In fact, we could argue that materialism is the *necessary* result of the postmodern view.

Why is it the necessary result? Simply because the only thing that the postmodernist can account for is what he can physically interact with; and even that, according to his presuppositions, borrows from Christianity.

Ultimate Morality

In a short summation then, the postmodernist rejects any sort of biding ultimate morality, and as we have seen already, must be his natural conclusion. It is because of his rejection of ultimate reality, ultimate authority, and a faulty epistemology that he ends up having no grounds, no basis for any sort of morality. Any morality, he would argue, is the result of myths or social constructs that can and will evolve with the natural passage of time. This is seen currently in our world with the devaluing and destruction of the family, rights of the unborn, freedom of speech, and the anti-biblical that gender and sex are not related or somehow fluid.

Final Analysis of Postmodernism

We have seen what the postmodernist "asserts."[81] As such, we must now put the whole system to the test against the truth found only in Christianity. In order to successfully test postmodernism, I want to borrow from Groothuis the various criteria he has laid out for such an evaluation.[82] The first point is that a worldview explains what it ought.[83] This seems simple enough, however, postmodernism fails in this category immediately. For example, as we have seen from postmodernism's rejection of reality, authority, and morality,

---

[81] It is rather doubtful that he would ever use the term, "believe."

[82] Groothuis, *Christian Apologetics*, 53-60. Here, he describes in detail eight criteria by which one may evaluate his worldview. We are only looking at four.

[83] Ibid., 53.

postmodernism cannot rightly account for any sort of pain or suffering within this world. Any attempt to argue otherwise from that position, the postmodernist derails his own assertions by contradiction.

Second, postmodernism struggles with the idea of existential viability.[84] On this, the postmodern worldview cannot sustain a consistent set of moral standards. That is, because everything that relates to the objectivity of belief and that matters of truth are relative, when the postmodernist is pushed for a defense, his views fail. He cannot hold on to his worldview *and* faithfully defend that rape, murder, incest, child abuse, and other heinous actions are morally wrong. This means that much like a naturalist, truth is lumped in together with what is beneficial. That is, a postmodernist *could* say that all of those things listed above are wrong, but he could not say it as a postmodernist.

Third, the postmodern view of the world fails with regard to cultural and intellectual development.[85] While it is possible to say that those engaged with postmodernism have been able to develop good aspects of culture as well as driving intellectualism forward, the postmodernist has done so in spite of himself. For example, one positive aspect of postmodernism is that the one who holds this view has been able to question various norms and boundaries that

---

[84] Ibid., 57.

[85] Ibid.

surround him.[86] In a sense, this is nothing more than healthy skepticism; it is what drives science and research. However, it has not done what it has intended; and that is it has not caused a reorientation or redefinition of truth. Some may object and point to the abortion industry—that the baby is not a baby until a certain point after conception—or the transgender movement—that a man can become a woman or vice versa—, but every science text will teach that it is *at* conception that a human is being formed and that while the externals may be changed, the DNA make up of a person is *either* male or female and therefore, not interchangeable. This is why when proponents of postmodernism profess that knowable, immutable truth is a myth, they cannot live it out practically.

The final point that we will use to evaluate postmodernism can be summed up by Occam's Razor. Groothuis writes, "Worldviews should not appeal to extraneous entities or be more complex than is required to explain what they propose to establish."[87] In short, if a worldview is unnecessarily complex, it does not mean that it should be the preferred view. This has to be the death knell on the postmodern view. The postmodernist may think that by abandoning all sense of truth and objectivity, seeking instead ultimate relativism is not all that complex an idea, however, what he has failed to realize is that by his pursuit

---

[86] L. Russ Bush, *The Advancement: Keeping the Faith in an Evolutionary Age* (Nashville, TN: B&H Publishing, 2003), 88.

[87] Groothuis, *Christian Apologetics*, 59.

to the absurd, he is left with needlessly complex consequences. For example, if the postmodern view is adopted in its entirety, there is no reason for something as essential to society as a just court system. With a mountain of evidence stacked against the accused, the judge could simply let the defendant walk for no reason, and no one would be able to justify their reasons why that was immoral.

Evaluation of Christianity

Since it has been shown that postmodernism fails in its attempts to provide a cohesive worldview, what then is the alternative? The only satisfactory alternative is the Christian worldview. Only Christianity has stood up to intense scrutiny and only Christianity will continue to do so. As such, we will see how the Christian view of the world compares to postmodernism under the same set of criteria from the above section. Using the first criteria, Christianity faithfully explains what it ought. In light of the concept of suffering and pain, only the Christian can make any sense of his duress and the duress of others in this life. For example, the Christian's highest example of purpose in suffering and pain is seen in the life of the Lord Jesus Christ. John writes in his Gospel that the Jews accused Jesus of blasphemy for claiming to be God (John 10:33). They sought to kill him as a result. Further, Jesus gave warnings to his disciples that because he was hated among men, they too, would be hated. "'If the world hates you, know that it has hated me before it hated you,'" (John 15:18).

However, Christ's greatest suffering came as a result of his passive obedience to death on a Roman cross. "No event of time or eternity compares with the transcending significance of the death of Christ on the cross."[88] While we do not have the space to go into great detail on this event, this great suffering produced a great good. As a result, the believer can be assured that while he may not understand the difficulties he is facing, the pain and suffering he is experiencing, that what some have intended for evil, God has intended for good.

Second, Christianity alone possesses consistent moral standards. Not only does Christianity possess these standards, it towers over all other worldviews, including postmodernism, by providing a consistent set of noncontradictory moral standards. Contrary to popular opinion, this consistency includes the Old and New Testaments. For example, after defining and defending the canon of Holy Scripture, the 1689 London Baptist Confession states, "The authority of the Holy Scripture, for which it ought to be believed, dependeth not upon the testimony of any man or church, but wholly upon God (who is truth itself), the Author thereof; therefore it is to be received because it is the Word of God."[89] The point of this declaration is that because we have reason to believe that God is the author of Scripture, and since God himself is the definitional, living truth, his Word cannot be inconsistent in any way, shape, or form.

---

[88] John F. Walvoord, *Jesus Christ Our Lord* (Chicago, IL: Moody Publishers, 1969), 153.

[89] Walter Chantry, ed., *The Baptist Confession of Faith 1689* (Carlisle, PA: The Banner of Truth Trust, 2017), 28.

Third, we can see that Christianity has been the shining beacon of cultural and intellectual development. No belief system in the history of the world has contributed more to the advancement of culture and intellect as Christianity. One only need look at European cathedrals, art, missions, adoption, modern hospitals and medical advancements, and universities to see the massive impact of the Christian religion. Perhaps the biggest impact on culture and intellect is the printing press. "The printing press was invented by the Christian man Johannes Gutenberg (1398-1468). Bibles and other Christian literature were chiefly in mind when he created the revolutionary device. Soon thereafter, Christianity became the leading force in literacy and education in the Western world."[90]

The final point that was used to evaluate postmodernism was the idea that the simplest explanation is often the best. It was shown that postmodernism fails extensively in this area. However, given the above three reasons in favor of Christianity, we can clearly assert that the simpler answer will indeed suffice. While postmodernism plays with the mind, bends the rules of logic, and is in a state of constant contradiction to make itself work, Christianity does the opposite.

For example, one of the simpler explanations as to

---

[90] Mark Driscoll and Gerry Breshears, *Vintage Jesus: Timely Answers to Timeless Questions* (Wheaton, IL: Crossway, 2007), 206. Now, while I am not in support of Driscoll and his doctrinal stances, this historical fact simply cannot be avoided.

how we can know God, and therefore know truth, is due to what Scripture records. John records that Jesus is the way, the truth, and the life (John 14:6). This claim is built on numerous examples revealed earlier in Scripture. Further, Christ's claim gives the structure to the 1689's confessional statement given earlier. The simple explanation is that God has revealed himself to his creation. The simple explanation is that God has revealed himself to be the author of truth. The simple explanation is that because God is infinite he can easily ensure that he truth is understandable. The simple explanation is that since God is God, we can trust him in all things on account of his very nature as God.

Defense of Christianity

Often when there is opposition to the Christian worldview, it stems from a misunderstanding of essential Christian beliefs that are rooted in Scripture. Two specific areas that are contested by the unbeliever, namely the postmodernist, are (1) theodicy, or the problem of evil, and (2) the resurrection of Jesus. We will look at each of these objections in turn, but it should be noted here that even in my best attempts to keep the arguments concise, entire books have been written on each of these subject.

Theodicy

The problem of evil is a sure problem for those not in Christ. How *can* evil exist when believers claim to follow an all-powerful, all-loving God who is in control of the universe? The problem with this question, however, is multifaceted. First, the person asking the question is neglecting a great truth of Christianity, and that is this: God is both holy *and* sovereign. Because God is holy, he can do no ill. Further, because God is sovereign, he can work—as with a tool in his hand—evil to accomplish his eternal plans. The 1689 declares:

> Although in relation to the foreknowledge and decree of God, the first cause, all things come to pass immutably and infallibly; so that there is not anything befalls any by chance, or without His providence; yet by the same providence He ordered them to fall out according to the nature of second causes, either necessarily, freely, or contingently.[91]

By this, it is to be understood that God is not the cause of evil, but can use evil through the nature of secondary causes to bring about his eternal decrees. The Belgic Confession of Faith records a similar truth. "God is neither the author of, nor can be charged with, the sins which are committed. For his power and goodness are so great and incomprehensible, that He orders and executes His work in the most excellent and just manner, even then when devils and wicked men act unjustly."[92] The confession continues that in some sense this is a mystery of the faith as

---

[91] Chantry, *1689*, 41.

[92] Netherlands Reformed Congregations, "The Belgic Confession," in *Doctrinal Standards, Liturgy, and Church Order* (Grand Rapids, MI: Netherlands Reformed Book and Publishing Committee, 2010), 11.

its fullness is incomprehensible.[93] A. W. Tozer asserts that, on this topic, God acted in accordance to his infinite wisdom and goodness.[94] In short: God ordains the means and ordains the ends of his purposes, and while doing so he remains sovereign and man remains responsible.

The Resurrection of Jesus

The resurrection of Jesus is the lynchpin of the Christian faith. The Apostle Paul says to the Corinthians, "And if Christ has not been raised, then our preaching is in vain and your faith is in vain," (1 Cor. 15:14). For the Christian, Scripture carries the most weight of evidence when studying the truth of the resurrection. In fact, the resurrection is the proof by which we rest our claims. After the resurrection, Jesus made multiple appearances to people before his ascension. On this, Groothuis lists them in rapid succession: Jesus appears to Mary Magdalene, to his mother Mary and other women, to Peter, to two disciples on the road to Emmaus, to ten of the apostles, then to the remaining eleven, again to seven, again to all the apostles, to another five hundred followers that might not have included women or children, to James his brother, and all of the apostles.[95] By quick estimation, it is likely that Jesus appeared to close to fifteen hundred followers before his ascension.

In sum, when we compare the Christian worldview to

93 Ibid.

94 A. W. Tozer, *The Knowledge of the Holy* (New York, NY: HarperOne, 1961), 110.

95 Groothuis, *Christian Apologetics*, 546.

postmodernism, postmodernism simply fails. Postmodernism cannot hold up under its own weight as it is fill of self-refuting claims and ever-changing definitions of truth, reality, morality, and authority. However, Christianity has not only stood the test of time and trial over the last two thousand years, it has also been shown to contain a set of coherent and cohesive arguments that are exclusive to the Christian faith. All of this while not violating any laws of logic. We have seen that even under close examination of some common objections to Christianity, the postmodernist's objections do not stand. God's goodness, holiness, and sovereignty, allows for evil in this world. God uses men and devils and their evil plotting like tools in the hands of a master craftsman. Further, the resurrection of Jesus is a proof rigorously documented inside and outside of Scripture. In light of this, postmodernism ought to be rejected as any sort of viable worldview while Christianity is to be warmly embraced.

ABOUT THE AUTHOR

Steven Capriglione is the author of several books and railroader. His goal for each of his works is that the reader would be blessed, encouraged, and challenged. He lives just outside of Grand Rapids, Michigan with his wife and two children.

www.ingramcontent.com/pod-product-compliance
Lightning Source LLC
Chambersburg PA
CBHW061443160726
47995CB00003B/1018